M000267594

THIS SKETCHBOOK BELONGS TO ....

CONTACT ....